ASTRONAUTS

Ryan Nagelhout

PowerKiDS press.

New York

Published in 2016 by The Rosen Publishing Group, Inc.
29 East 21st Street, New York, NY 10010

First Edition

Editor: Katie Kawa
Designer: Mickey Harmon

Photo Credits: Cover Marc Ward/Shutterstock.com; pp. 4–5 NASA/Handout/Getty Images; pp. 6–7, 13 (space) pixelparticle/Shutterstock.com; p. 7 (inset) Photo 12/Contributor/Universal Images Group Editorial/Getty Images; pp. 8–9 Science & Society Picture Library/Contributor/SSPL/Getty Images; p. 9 (inset) https:// upload.wikimedia.org/wikipedia/commons/a/a8/Mission_Control_celebrates_ successful_splashdown_of_Apollo_13.jpg; pp. 10–11 Space Frontiers/Stringer/ Archive Photos/Getty Images; p. 13 (astronaut) Vadim Sadovski/Shutterstock.com; p. 14 Alexanderphoto7/Shutterstock.com; pp. 14–15, 18–19, 22–23, 24–25, 26 (inset) courtesy of NASA; p. 17 SCIENCE SOURCE/Science Source/Getty Images; p. 21 (main) FotograFFF/Shutterstock.com; p. 21 (inset) Vacclav/ Shutterstock.com; p. 23 (inset) https://en.wikipedia.org/wiki/Chris_Hadfield#/ media/File:Chris_Hadfield_2011.jpg; pp. 26–27 Tristan3D/Shutterstock.com; pp. 28–29 Triff/Shutterstock.com; p. 30 Juergen Faelchle/Shutterstock.com.

Cataloging-in-Publication Data

Nagelhout, Ryan.
Astronauts / by Ryan Nagelhout.
p. cm. — (Out of the lab: extreme jobs in science)
Includes index.
ISBN 978-1-5081-4509-7 (pbk.)
ISBN 978-1-5081-4510-3 (6-pack)
ISBN 978-1-5081-4511-0 (library binding)
1. Astronautics — Juvenile literature. 2. Astronauts — Juvenile literature. I.
Nagelhout, Ryan. II. Title.
TL793.N34 2016
629.45—d23

Manufactured in the United States of America

CPSIA Compliance Information: Batch #BW16PK: For Further Information contact Rosen Publishing, New York, New York at 1-800-237-9932

Contents

Science Takes Off 4

The First Class 6

The Moon and Back 8

Schmitt's Legacy 10

What It Takes 12

Passing the Tests 16

Study Hard! 18

Playing a Part 20

Life in Space 22

Space Experiments......................... 24

A Year in Space.............................. 26

Life After Flight.............................. 28

Science in Space 30

Glossary... 31

Index.. 32

Websites... 32

SCIENCE TAKES OFF

A love of science can take you to many extreme places. Being a researcher often means leaving the laboratory and exploring the world. Scientists search the deepest depths of the ocean looking for new life. They study in the **intense** heat of volcanoes and the deadly cold of Antarctica. They even test new technology that can save millions of lives.

Did you know science can take you into space? Astronauts are living and working in space right now! Do you think you have what it takes to study science in space? You have to be smart, strong, and willing to leave your friends and family for a long time. It's not easy, but the view from above Earth is worth the tough training. Read on to find out what it takes to be an astronaut!

SCIENCE IN ACTION

In the United States, an astronaut is a person who travels into space as part of the National **Aeronautics** and Space Administration (NASA). A cosmonaut is an astronaut in the Russian space program.

The word "astronaut" comes from the Greek words for "space sailor."

THE FIRST CLASS

The first astronauts weren't scientists; they were pilots. NASA needed people with flight experience to guide the first missions to and from space. In 1959, NASA asked the U.S. military to list members of the armed forces who fit a certain list of qualifications. NASA was getting ready for its first manned space mission, which took place in 1961. It needed astronauts qualified to take humankind into space.

NASA asked for military men who had flown jet aircraft and had some engineering experience. They couldn't be taller than 5 feet 11 inches (180 cm) because of limited space inside the Mercury **space capsule**. After a number of tests and trials, NASA picked seven men out of the 500 who applied to be astronauts.

SCIENCE IN ACTION

The first person in space was Russian cosmonaut Yuri Gagarin. He was successfully launched into space on April 12, 1961.

Shown here are the first seven NASA astronauts. These space pioneers weren't scientists, but they helped change the way we understand space science.

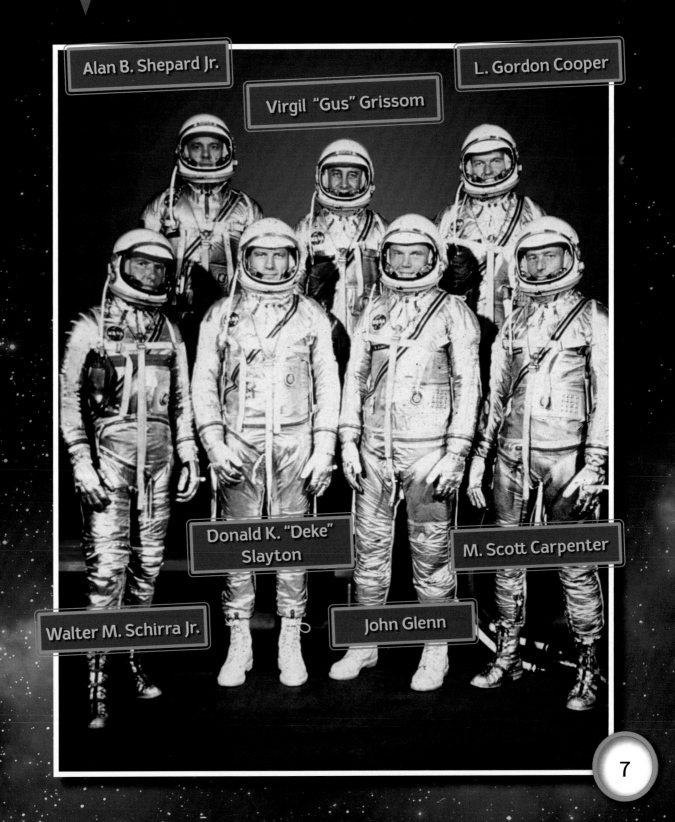

Alan B. Shepard Jr.

Virgil "Gus" Grissom

L. Gordon Cooper

Donald K. "Deke" Slayton

M. Scott Carpenter

Walter M. Schirra Jr.

John Glenn

THE MOON AND BACK

In 1961, Alan B. Shepard Jr. became the first American in space. Shepard's flight lasted 15 minutes and went 116 miles (186.7 km) high in Earth's atmosphere. Throughout the 1960s, NASA's Mercury and Gemini programs continued to test astronauts' ability to travel through space.

The Apollo program, which was first publicly talked about in 1961, was created to put men on the moon. The first Apollo mission ended in tragedy. Three astronauts—including Gus Grissom—died in a fire during a preflight test in 1967.

Two years later, though, *Apollo 11* landed on the moon. The last Apollo mission was *Apollo 17*, which took place in December 1972. Just 12 men walked on the moon's surface in the six successful Apollo moon landings. Astronauts conducted experiments and collected moon rocks, which they brought back to Earth to be studied.

SCIENCE IN ACTION

On July 20, 1969, Neil Armstrong became the first astronaut to walk on the moon. The last astronaut to walk on the moon to date was Eugene Cernan in 1972.

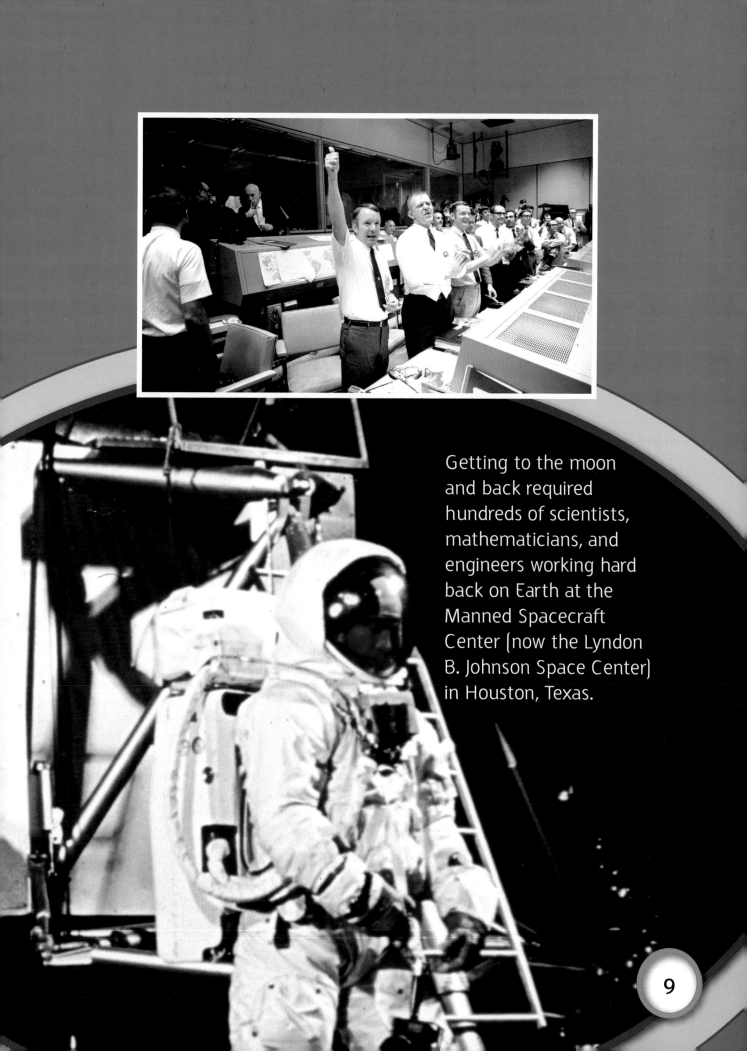

Getting to the moon and back required hundreds of scientists, mathematicians, and engineers working hard back on Earth at the Manned Spacecraft Center (now the Lyndon B. Johnson Space Center) in Houston, Texas.

SCHMITT'S LEGACY

Harrison Schmitt is the only scientist to ever walk on the moon to date. Schmitt was a geologist who went to space with the *Apollo 17* mission. He received a **doctorate** degree in geology from Harvard University in 1964. In 1965, Schmitt was chosen by NASA to be a scientist-astronaut.

Schmitt's flight training came next. He took a 53-week flight training course to catch up with other astronauts. He retired with more than 2,100 hours of flying time, with 1,600 of those hours spent in a jet. Schmitt was a late addition to the *Apollo 17* crew because of his scientific experience. Astronauts don't visit the moon anymore, but today's scientist-astronauts are more closely related to Schmitt than the other Apollo astronauts.

Harrison Schmitt, shown here, helped pave the way for future scientists in space.

WHAT IT TAKES

Schmitt was the first scientist-astronaut. In time, NASA's missions focused more on science than they did before. Newer astronaut applicants needed college degrees and years of experience in science, math, or engineering. About half of NASA's astronauts have an engineering background. Others have degrees in medicine, chemistry, biology, and other branches of science. No two astronauts have the exact same background.

It's still not easy to get into space today. NASA only picks a new class of astronauts as they're needed. Out of the thousands of people who apply to be an astronaut candidate, only a small number are selected.

Getting named an astronaut candidate is just the start. What follows is a two-year training period that not everyone finishes.

SCIENCE IN ACTION

All NASA astronauts must be U.S. citizens. Different countries' space programs have different requirements for their astronauts.

NASA astronaut requirements

good blood pressure (not more than 140/90 in sitting position)

three years of practical experience in their field

at least a bachelor's degree in science, engineering, or math

height between 62 and 75 inches (157 and 191 cm)

U.S. citizenship

1,000 hours piloting jet aircraft (for pilots and commanders)

20/20 vision

Astronaut candidates must meet many educational and physical requirements before being chosen to begin training.

There are two different kinds of astronaut applications. The first is a military application. These vary depending on what branch of the military a person serves in, but the applications are handled through the armed forces. Civilians, or people not in the military, apply directly to NASA through a government jobs website. NASA officials look over the applications and pick the top applicants to interview in person.

Finalists are interviewed, and they also go through medical screenings, or tests. Astronauts have a **dangerous** job, so NASA needs to know it's chosen the best people possible for this line of work. Only the most physically and mentally prepared people can handle such an extreme career path.

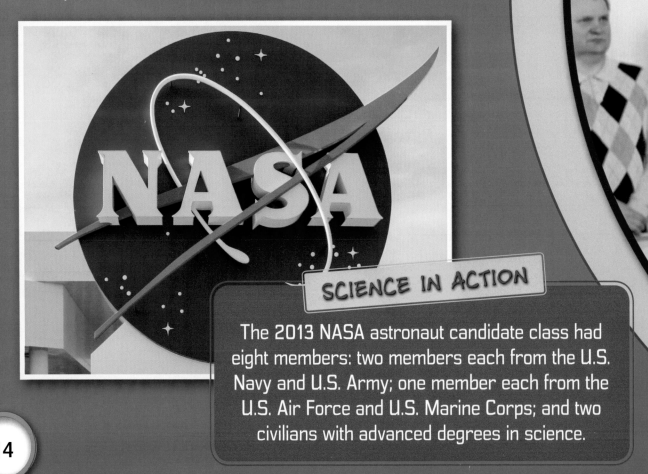

SCIENCE IN ACTION

The 2013 NASA astronaut candidate class had eight members: two members each from the U.S. Navy and U.S. Army; one member each from the U.S. Air Force and U.S. Marine Corps; and two civilians with advanced degrees in science.

Many people have to apply multiple times before they're accepted into the astronaut candidate program. Astronauts say you can't take no for an answer!

15

PASSING THE TESTS

Just because someone is picked for astronaut training doesn't mean they're an astronaut yet. Astronaut candidates get assigned to the Astronaut Office at the Johnson Space Center. For the next two years, they undergo intense training to see if they can make it in space. Candidates get basic military water survival training. They then have to pass a swimming test that involves swimming laps in a space suit. Candidates also have to **tread** water for 10 minutes in the suit.

The NASA swimming test is important because training for **spacewalks** takes place underwater. Astronauts must also get **SCUBA** training, and they learn to deal with high and low air pressure, which they may experience in space. Changes in air pressure can affect the human body, so astronauts need to be prepared for these changes.

SCIENCE IN ACTION

Astronaut candidates practice flying in jets that make them feel weightless for about 20 seconds. This extreme training sometimes happens up to 40 times a day!

Civilians who don't pass the many tests to become astronauts are sometimes given other jobs with NASA, but they aren't allowed to travel into space. Only candidates who pass these tests can handle the extreme forces of space travel.

STUDY HARD!

Becoming an astronaut isn't just about physical training. Astronaut candidates have to hit the books, too! NASA astronauts study the many systems they may use aboard different kinds of spacecraft. Astronauts also go through computer-based training for potential problems they may have in space. They need to know how to handle a problem with any system on the spacecraft.

Once astronauts are assigned to a flight mission, their training may take up to three years. Astronauts often learn to use a robotic arm to perform tasks outside the spacecraft. They can learn to conduct spacewalks or how to perform experiments related to their science or engineering degrees.

Astronauts have to learn to live in space, too. Life in space isn't easy. Astronauts learn to make meals, sleep, and even go to the bathroom in space!

SCIENCE IN ACTION

Astronauts learn to use the bathroom in space before they're sent on their missions. They use a space toilet, which has loops for their feet. This keeps them from floating away while using the toilet because of weightlessness in space.

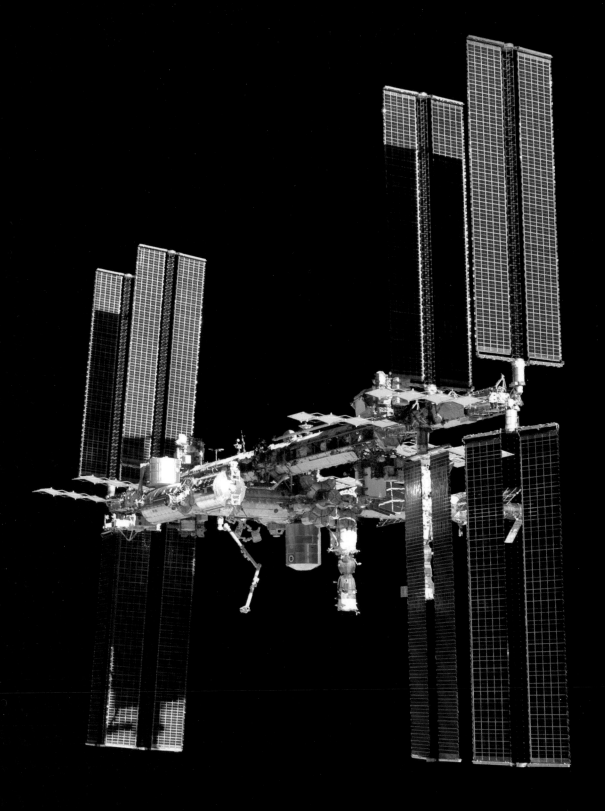

NASA astronauts often train for missions that take place aboard the International Space Station (ISS). Astronauts must learn to speak Russian before traveling to the ISS.

PLAYING A PART

Every astronaut has a different role on a mission. Astronauts receive different training to perform each role. The commander is in charge of each mission and the safety of the crew. The pilot guides space **vehicles** and the ISS. The pilot also helps the mission commander.

Mission specialists work with the commander to complete a mission's special goals. They're trained to complete work outside the ISS, repairing or adding new parts to the station. They also help perform experiments using a robotic arm.

Payload specialists are people other than NASA astronauts that have a special role in a mission. While payload specialists aren't astronauts, they still have to meet physical and educational requirements. They also go through intense training related to their mission or specific experiment.

SCIENCE IN ACTION

Astronauts often travel to foreign countries to train with other space programs. The U.S. and the Russian space programs were once considered rivals, but now astronauts and cosmonauts work together aboard the ISS.

NASA's Space Shuttle program was retired in 2011. This means current astronauts often travel to and from the ISS on Russian Soyuz spacecraft.

SOYUZ SPACECRAFT

SPACE SHUTTLE

LIFE IN SPACE

The first piece of the ISS was sent into orbit in 1998. It took more than 10 years and 30 different missions to put this space station together. The ISS travels at 17,500 miles (28,163.5 km) per hour to keep the 460-ton (417 mt) station in orbit about 240 miles (386 km) above Earth's surface. As of 2015, 16 countries have used the ISS for scientific experiments.

Astronauts living on the ISS make sure the station is working properly at all times. Sometimes they have to go out into space wearing a space suit in order to check on or repair a part of the station. Astronauts on the ISS also need to exercise every day. If they don't exercise, their body will weaken because there's less gravity on the ISS than on Earth.

SCIENCE IN ACTION

Most of the food astronauts eat is **freeze-dried**. However, they can bring fresh food into space as long as they eat it before it spoils.

Astronauts have to find creative ways to fill their spare time in space. Canadian astronaut Chris Hadfield played guitar while on the ISS. He even made a music video from space!

CHRIS HADFIELD

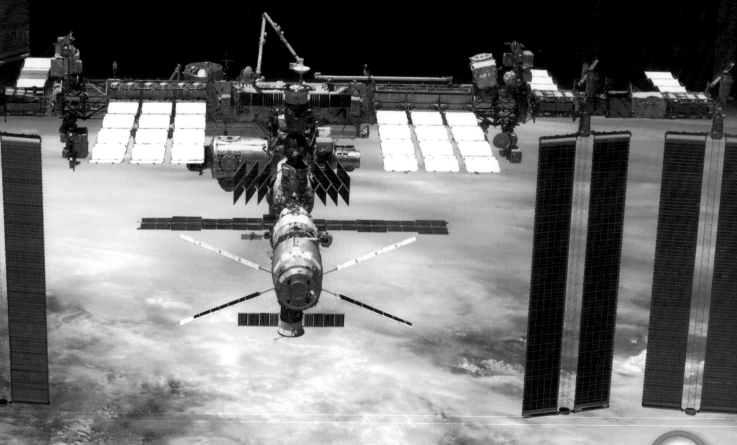

SPACE EXPERIMENTS

The biggest advantage of doing science experiments aboard the ISS is microgravity, or the condition of weightlessness in space. The pull of gravity is weaker on the ISS than on Earth. This lets astronauts float! They often push or pull themselves through the ISS with their hands because they can't walk. Astronauts do experiments with human cells, animal body parts, and even very small living things in microgravity.

Different scientists perform different experiments in space. Physical scientists study how the human body reacts to low gravity, while engineers test new technology to keep the ISS running properly. Astronauts even take photographs of Earth's glaciers, cities, coral reefs, and other features from the ISS. These photos are used to study Earth in ways scientists on the surface of the planet can't.

SCIENCE IN ACTION

Because of the weakened force of gravity in space, fluids travel in an astronaut's body from their legs to their head. This might make an astronaut's face look swollen, but it doesn't cause any real harm.

Experiments done aboard the ISS help astronauts live in space, and they help us on Earth, too.

One of the most interesting experiments in the history of the ISS started on March 27, 2015. On that date, NASA astronaut Scott Kelly went into space with the mission of staying aboard the ISS for a full year. This was meant to test how the body reacts to long-term space travel.

Scott's twin brother, Mark, is a retired astronaut. During Scott's year in space, Mark stayed on Earth. The twins were tested and their results were compared to measure the effect living in space has on the human body.

Scott and Mark both had their blood, **urine**, and **feces** tested during the year. They were also put through a number of physical and mental tests. This extreme space experiment was designed to find out how an astronaut's body might be affected by a mission to Mars.

MARK KELLY   SCOTT KELLY

The Kelly twins were chosen to help NASA prepare for future missions to Mars and other far-out places in space. Scott said he was excited "to do as much science on this flight as I can."

A trip to Mars could last 500 days or longer, and NASA wants to know how dangerous a mission that long would be for its astronauts.

LIFE AFTER FLIGHT

Life on Earth can be hard for returning astronauts. Getting used to gravity again can make them feel dizzy or sick. A few weeks in space might make astronauts **queasy** for a few days after returning to Earth. After six months in space, though, astronauts might take a few weeks to get used to Earth again.

Even when astronauts aren't in space, they're constantly working on other missions. Those not assigned to fly on a mission help others prepare for their time in space. Astronauts help other NASA scientists develop experiments to conduct aboard the ISS, and they work to make sure the equipment astronauts will use in space is ready for flight. Some astronauts work in Mission Control at the Johnson Space Center, helping NASA monitor astronauts and experiments in space.

SCIENCE IN ACTION

NASA says it doesn't have plans to send children into space right now. However, kids may be able to travel into space in the future as new technology makes space travel easier and safer.

An astronaut's job is extreme both in space and on Earth!

SCIENCE IN SPACE

Being an astronaut isn't an easy career path. It's dangerous, it's hard work, and it's a tough job to get. However, if you do become an astronaut, you'll have the chance to do important work in an amazing setting. The work astronauts do doesn't just change the way we understand our planet; it can change the way we understand the universe.

If you dream of leaving Earth, you need to start preparing now. Work hard in school, especially in science and math classes. With a lot of studying and training, you could have the chance to use science in space. You might even use science to travel to Mars in the future!

GLOSSARY

aeronautics: The science of flight.

dangerous: Not safe.

doctorate: The highest degree given by a university.

feces: Solid waste from a person or animal's body.

freeze-dried: Frozen quickly to remove liquid in order to allow something such as food to last longer.

intense: Existing to an extreme degree.

queasy: Having a sick feeling in the stomach.

SCUBA: An acronym for Self Contained Underwater Breathing Apparatus, which is technology used to allow people to breathe underwater.

space capsule: A small spacecraft that is part of a larger spacecraft that holds instruments or crew.

spacewalk: A period of activity spent outside a spacecraft by an astronaut in space.

tread: To keep the body nearly upright in water and the head above water using a walking motion.

urine: Liquid waste from a person or animal's body.

vehicle: A machine used to carry people or goods from one place to another.

INDEX

A
Apollo 11, 8
Apollo 17, 8, 10
Armstrong, Neil, 8

B
biology, 12

C
candidates, 12, 13, 14, 15,
    16, 18
chemistry, 12
commander, 20
cosmonaut, 4, 6, 20

E
engineering, 6, 9, 12, 13,
    18, 24
experiments, 8, 18, 20,
    22, 24, 25, 26, 28

G
Gagarin, Yuri, 6
Gemini program, 8
geology, 10
Grissom, Gus, 7, 8

I
ISS, 19, 20, 22, 23, 24,
    25, 26, 28

K
Kelly, Scott and
    Mark, 26

L
Lyndon B. Johnson
    Space Center,
    9, 16, 28

M
math, 9, 12, 13, 30
Mercury program, 6, 8
mission specialists, 20
moon, 8, 9, 10, 11

N
NASA, 4, 6, 7, 8, 10,
    12, 14, 16, 18, 19,
    20, 26, 27, 28

P
payload specialists, 20
pilot, 6, 20

R
requirements, 12, 13, 20

S
Schmitt, Harrison, 10,
    11, 12
Shepard, Alan B., Jr., 7, 8

T
training, 4, 10, 12, 13, 16,
    18, 20, 30

WEBSITES

Due to the changing nature of Internet links, PowerKids Press has developed an online list of websites related to the subject of this book. This site is updated regularly. Please use this link to access the list:
www.powerkidslinks.com/exsci/astro